INTRODUCTION

The day-to-day life of any student in fashion school can be hectic: rushing to classes, laying out pattern pieces, unpicking wonky stitch lines, working towards meeting imminent deadlines, choosing art materials, doing research late at night in the library. Wherever you are, you are guaranteed to hear snippets of conversation – nuggets of fashion wisdom – but may be too busy to take it all in. The tips and advice in this book bring together the experience of more informed fashion students, fashion lecturers and technical staff, such as pattern cutters and machinists, so you can dip in at your leisure, ensuring you get the most out of being at fashion school.

EZINMA MBONU

CONTENTS

1 Presenting your research

2 Drawing topstitching

3 Sticking imagery in your sketchbook

4 Different sized sketchbooks

5 Mark-making techniques

6 Karl Lagerfeld

7 Improve your time management

8 Rip fabric along the grain line

9 Put your name on your portfolio

10 Start your own personal library

11 Womenswear fastens right over left

12 Coco Chanel

13 Matching threads to fabric

14 Modeling garments for presentation

15 Nervous about presenting?

16 Silhouette

17 Combining different fabrics

18 Mary Quant

19 Vintage and thrift stores

20 The bias

21 Constructive criticism

22 Testing art media

23 Practise machining straight lines

24 Yves Saint-Laurent

25 Bagging garments out

26 Give your fashion drawings hands

27 Start a fabric library

28 Consider different fastenings

29 Miuccia Prada

30 Making good eye contact

31 Draw from life

32 Fashion illustrations are nine heads

33 Different types of pocket

34 Yohji Yamamoto

35 Develop your initial design ideas

36 Showcasing fabric swatches

37 Alexander McQueen

38 Cutting chiffon

39 Pattern-cutting table

40 Presentation sheet templates

41 Vivienne Westwood

42 Use a photocopier creatively

43 Go window-shopping

44 Pattern pieces and fabric pile

45 Limit eraser use in sketchbooks

46 The warp of the fabric

47 Orson Wells

48 Proportion

49 Clean your portfolio

50 Get involved

51 Always remove dressmaking pins

52 Avoid too many black and white photocopies

53 Lady Gaga

FASHION

SCHOOL

SURVIVAL

Guide

EZINMA MBONU

Published in 2015
by Laurence King Publishing Ltd
361–373 City Road
London EC1V 1LR
Tel +44 20 7841 6900
Fax +44 20 7841 6910
E enquiries@laurenceking.com
www.laurenceking.com

Design ©2015 Laurence King Publishing Ltd
Text ©2015 Ezinma Mbonu
Illustrations ©2015 Anna Hammer and
Ayako Koyama
Designed by Masumi Briozzo
Project editor: Gaynor Sermon

A catalogue record for this book is available from
the British Library

ISBN 978 178067 607 4
Printed in China

LAURENCE KING

54 Give your fashion drawings faces
55 Different types of collar
56 Buy or make a sketchbook?
57 Buy a sketchbook with fewer pages than you can fill
58 Always read around your research topic
59 Sewing leather
60 Diana Vreeland
61 Draw, draw and draw some more
62 Happy feet
63 Where to place zips/zippers
64 Best direction for button holes
65 Use a fixative on soft art media
66 Ralph Lauren
67 Style lines
68 Include shoes in your fashion drawings
69 Don't forget to include darts in your flats
70 Long, narrow skirts
71 Don't forget fabric swatches in your sketchbook
72 The warp of the fabric
73 Anna Wintour
74 Pleats
75 Separate scissors for cutting paper and fabric
76 Create a template for a fashion drawing
77 Securing pattern pieces

78 The grain line
79 Oscar Wilde
80 Always add a seam allowance
81 Practise your presentation
82 Find out how wide the fabric is
83 Magnets
84 Templates for each project in your portfolio
85 Jean Cocteau
86 Zips/zippers
87 Collect inspiring things
88 Ensure symmetry with hand-drawn flats
89 The right side of the fabric
90 There's no such word as can't
91 Avoid using soft pencils for fashion drawings
92 When drawing flats, keep garments in proportion
93 Avoid printing lo-res imagery
94 Centre-front and centre-back seams
95 Womenswear sizing: dresses, jackets and coats
96 Menswear sizing: suits, jackets and coats
97 Menswear: trousers
98 Menswear: dress shirts
99 Womens shoe sizes
100 Mens shoe sizes

DON'T LABOUR OVER EVERY INDIVIDUAL BIT OF RESEARCH IMAGERY WHEN PRESENTING.

Focus on key elements of your research and summarize. Have you ever listened to a fellow student present their design project and tried very hard to stay awake? Sometimes it is not the project itself that is boring, but the length of time that the student is taking to explain their design process. Grab everyone's attention by presenting a concise overview of your project, highlighting key points within your process that have informed your research and final outcome.

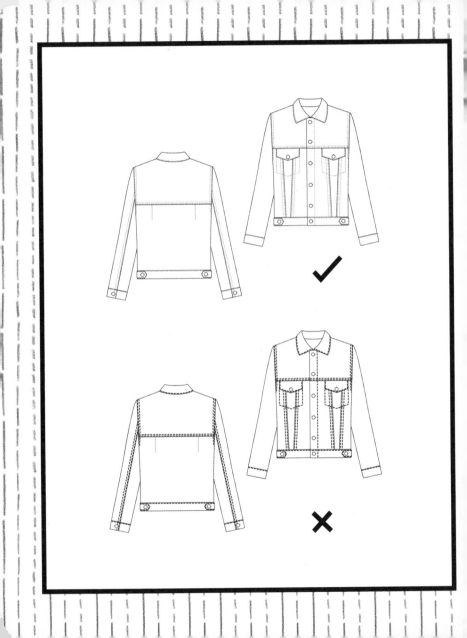

WHEN DRAWING TOPSTITCHING KEEP IT IN PROPORTION,

don't make it monster sized! Topstitching is a stitch line sewn on the right side of the fabric that is situated parallel to the seam line (hem line, cuff or other edge). It can be used as a decorative finish, but often its purpose is functional. It can transform a garment from looking homemade to something that looks more professional. A common mistake when drawing flats (technical drawings) that have a topstitch detail is to unintentionally exaggerate the proportion of the topstitch in relation to the rest of the drawn garment. The best way to indicate a topstitch on a flat is to draw a faint (compared to the weight of line used elsewhere) continuous line.

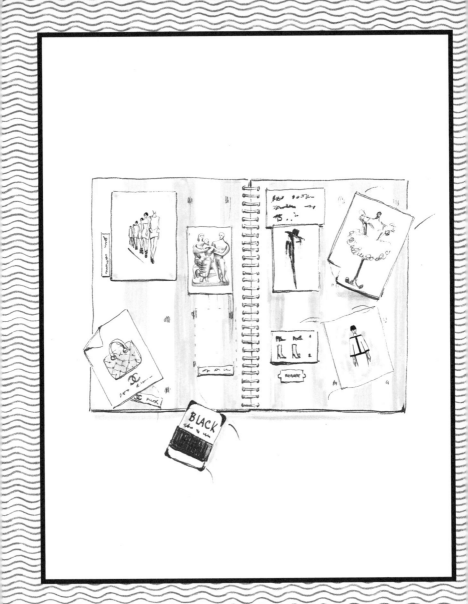

CHOOSE A GOOD ADHESIVE FOR STICKING YOUR RESEARCH IMAGERY INTO YOUR SKETCHBOOK.

It is best to avoid water-based glues as they tend to create air pockets between the layers over time. Some glues curl pages due to thickness and others lose stickiness over time – this can happen with some aerosol adhesives. Look for specialist craft glue, making sure it's right for your purposes.

EXPERIMENT WITH DIFFERENT SIZED SKETCHBOOKS.

Sketchbooks of varying sizes, with different orientations (landscape or portrait) are widely available. Typically you will find yourself using A3, A4 or A5 (in the US 8.5 x 11 in, 11 x 17 in or 5 x 8 in). Don't just stick to one size, experiment with different sizes and orientations to work out which one suits you best.

charcoal

pencil

watercolour

EXPERIMENT WITH DIFFERENT MARK-MARKING TECHNIQUES.

Get to know your individual media. How many different types of mark can you make using a stick of charcoal? Which different media do you think work well together?

'One is never overdressed or underdressed with a Little Black Dress.'

KARL LAGERFELD

SEPTEMBER

MON	TUE	WED	THU	FRI	SAT	SUN
	1 *Briefing meeting 10am*	2	3	4	5	6
7	8	9	10	11	12	13
14	15	16	17	18 *Deadline!!!*	19	20
21	22	23	24	25	26	27
28	29	30				

IMPROVE YOUR TIME MANAGEMENT FOR PROJECTS

by drawing up your own timetable to work in
conjunction with the project's timetable. Working
backward from the submission date can really
help you in moving forward. By doing this you
can allocate a window of time for all the research
and development stages, working backward to
when you first received your design brief. Stick
to it, otherwise there would be no point in
drawing it up.

IT IS OFTEN EASY TO RIP FABRIC ALONG THE GRAIN LINE.

Some fabrics, such as cotton, are easy to divide
into smaller lengths by simply ripping them,
after a little snip from a pair of scissors to get
you started. This is less time consuming
than using a pair of scissors.

DON'T FORGET TO PUT YOUR NAME ON YOUR PORTFOLIO – INSIDE AND OUTSIDE.

Can you imagine not receiving an assessment mark because of this? It's a common mistake. To avoid this happening include this entry in a checklist that you should create ahead of any submission, just to ensure that you have all of the required components.

START YOU OWN PERSONAL LIBRARY OF INSPIRATIONAL BOOKS.

Books are an invaluable research resource.
It makes perfect sense to establish this resource
at home, so that you can have around the clock
access. This need not be a costly venture either.
Libraries tend to have periodic clearances – where
books are either free or being sold off cheaply.
There are also many websites and bookstores
that specialize in secondhand books.

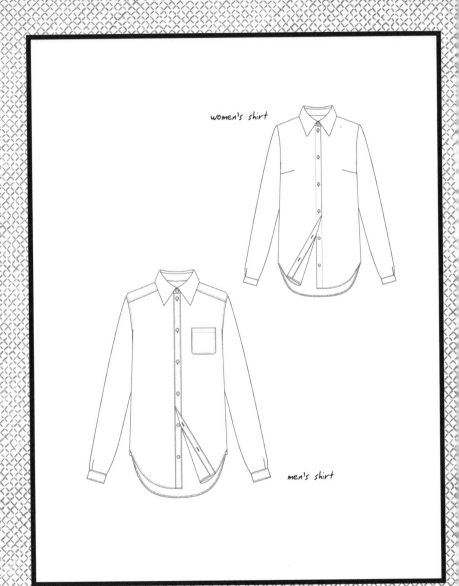

women's shirt

men's shirt

11

WOMEN ARE ALWAYS RIGHT! WHEN IT COMES TO CLOTHING, WOMENSWEAR FASTENS RIGHT OVER LEFT.

Have you ever noticed that men's and women's shirts, jackets, coats and trousers button differently? On menswear the buttons are on the right, on womenswear they are on the left. The most widely accepted reason for this is because most people are right-handed: historically women who could afford clothing with many buttons had maids to dress them, so the buttons were on the right-hand side for the maid's benefit and on the wearer's left. Men, on the other hand, generally dressed themselves.

'I don't do fashion, I AM fashion.'

COCO CHANEL

WHEN MATCHING THREADS TO A LENGTH OF FABRIC, CHOOSE THE DARKER TONE.

There are so many different colours that matching the right colour thread to a particular fabric can be very confusing. Under a good light draw out thread from three reels that appear to be the closest in colour and tone. Place them on top of the fabric for comparison. When sewn, the darker tone always looks more professional.

14

WHEN YOU HAVE MADE A GARMENT, ALWAYS GET SOMEONE TO MODEL IT FOR PRESENTATIONS.

Not all garments have hanger appeal. However, all garments should look better on the human form than on a hanger, otherwise what is the point?! Clothes never look good when they are too tight and the seams are bulging – always aim for slightly roomy rather than too tight. Make sure your chosen model shows your garment at its best. Going one step further and accessorizing will help to achieve this.

15

NERVOUS ABOUT PRESENTING?

If possible, find the room where the presentation is to be held and spend some time there in order to familiarize yourself with the environment. We have all felt the fear of the unknown. Presenting in front of your group and tutors can be nerve-wracking enough, let alone presenting in an unfamiliar environment. The best way to keep nerves at bay is to, as far as is possible, make the unfamiliar familiar.

16

SILHOUETTE.

In fashion this refers to the outline of a
garment or outfit. Fashionable silhouettes change
frequently according to the current vogue.
Historically, certain periods and, more recently,
even decades can be defined by the favoured
silhouette of the time.

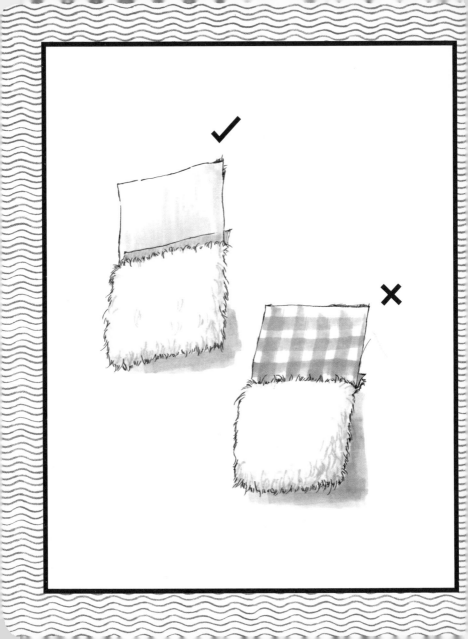

17

WHEN COMBINING DIFFERENT FABRICS, ALWAYS MAKE SAMPLES

to ensure that the different characteristics of each fabric work together. Mixing fabrics can add a lot of interest to a garment. To ensure that you make the right choices you need to experiment with your fabric lengths. There are fabric combinations that really do not work and others that are perfect – set aside some time to make the discovery.

'Good taste is death. Vulgarity is life.'

MARY QUANT

FIND OUT WHERE YOUR NEAREST VINTAGE AND THRIFT STORES ARE

– they are great for inspiration and research! Looking at how fabrics, details, fastenings, cut and silhouette have been used over the decades up-close and personal can be truly inspiring.

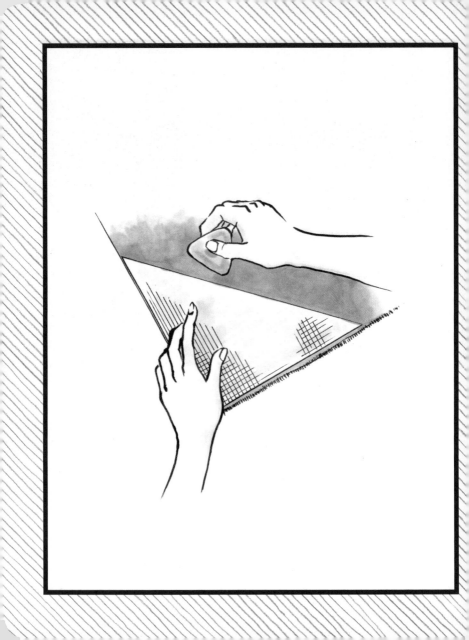

20

THE BIAS RUNS AT A 45-DEGREE ANGLE FROM THE WEFT AND WARP.

A good way to discover the bias in a piece of fabric is to use a set square (triangle) and some chalk. Place one of the shorter edges of the set square against the selvedge of the fabric. The hypotenuse (the longest side) represents the bias. Mark this gently with chalk and remove the set square to reveal the bias grain.

DON'T TAKE CRITIQUE PERSONALLY. CONSTRUCTIVE CRITICISM HELPS YOU TO IMPROVE UPON YOUR WORK.

The fashion industry is one that requires you to have a 'thick skin'; it is not the best place to wear your heart on your sleeve. Learning how to take constructive criticism on the chin is essential to survival in the industry. Constructive criticism is not to be seen as an attack on the standard of your work. The point of a critique is to flag up areas for further improvement.

22

WHEN TESTING OUT NEW ART MEDIA AVOID BUYING LARGE BOX SETS.

Buy a sample (an individual piece) first. See if new media suits you before investing in a box set. When you start a new course the temptation is to buy absolutely everything that you might possibly need. Art media can be pretty pricey, and there is so much to choose from. Experiment first with a variety of samples to understand your preferences.

PRACTISE MACHINE SEWING STRAIGHT PARALLEL STITCH LINES,

some very close to each other, others with more distance apart. The only way to improve the look of your sewing and correct wonky stitch lines is to practise, practise, practise until the stitch lines are completely straight and perfect.

'Fashions fade, style is eternal.'

YVES SAINT-LAURENT

WHEN BAGGING GARMENTS OUT, MAKE SURE THAT YOU HAVE ALLOWED SUFFICIENT SPACE TO FEED FABRIC THROUGH.

Bagging out is when two layers of pattern pieces are sewn together inside out (with the wrong side of the fabric on the outside) along the circumference, leaving a small gap so that the right side of the fabric can be pulled through. This method is used frequently when making cushions, and with some garments.

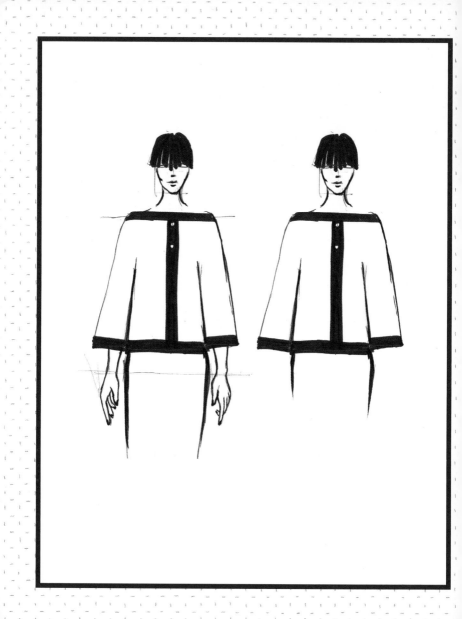

26

GIVE YOUR FASHION DRAWINGS HANDS – IT HELPS TO GET A SENSE OF PROPORTION WITH SLEEVE LENGTH.

Even if drawing hands is one of your pet hates, it is essential to at least give an indication in your drawings. Otherwise it is difficult to tell whether the sleeves drawn are just above the wrist, three-quarter length, or overly long.

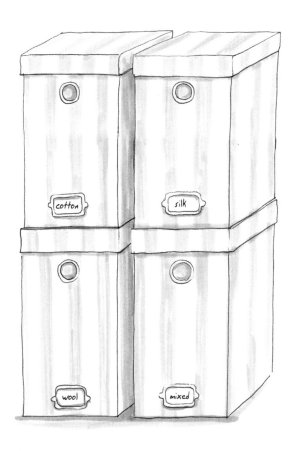

27

START A FABRIC LIBRARY.

What to do with the growing pile of fabric swatches that you have collected over several visits to fabric shops but don't currently need? Starting a fabric library is the perfect solution. This can be created using a folder where you separate swatches into different fibre types, so they can be easily found again when needed. Or you could separate fibres into different box files, depending on the space you have available.

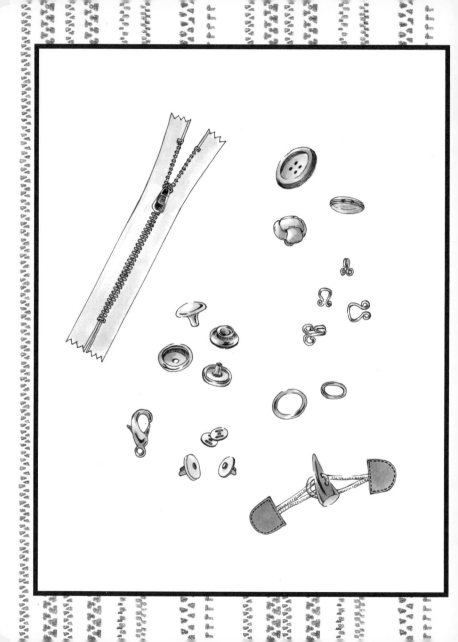

ALWAYS CONSIDER DIFFERENT TYPES OF FASTENING DURING YOUR DESIGN PROCESS,

don't leave this until the end. Fastenings can be an integral part of the design if considered earlier on in the research and development stages.

'What you wear is
how you present
yourself to the world,
especially today,
when human contacts
are so quick. Fashion
is instant language.'

MIUCCIA PRADA

IT'S ALL ABOUT MAKING GOOD EYE CONTACT.

All the time that you have spent researching, designing, pattern cutting and sewing a garment has been geared up to the project deadline – the presentation. Key to every good presentation is good eye contact. It conveys confidence, a knowledge of your subject and also your desire to engage your audience.

DRAW FROM LIFE AS OFTEN AS YOU CAN TO HONE YOUR OBSERVATIONAL SKILLS.

The ability to observe and interpret what you see is at the heart of fashion design. From observational drawing you gain an understanding of proportion, scale and texture.

FASHION ILLUSTRATIONS ARE NINE HEADS.

Fashion illustrations typically show clothes on an elongated figure. It is widely accepted that the average person is approximately seven heads long: that is, their overall height is divisible by the length of their head into seven parts. In the case of the fashion illustration, the figure is stretched so that it is divisible into nine parts – the length of nine heads. This results in a figure with elongated limbs, providing more surface area to show off designs and design details.

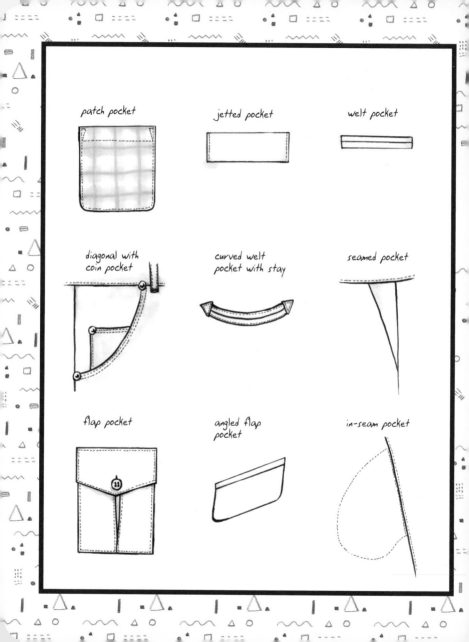

patch pocket

jetted pocket

welt pocket

diagonal with coin pocket

curved welt pocket with stay

seamed pocket

flap pocket

angled flap pocket

in-seam pocket

33

DIFFERENT TYPES OF POCKET.

A pocket is best described as a pouch or receptacle that is closed at one end, in order to hold something. They are found either on the outside or inside of a garment. Pockets can be decorative as well as functional. Create your own reference library by buying cheap garments with a variety of pockets at a flea market or yard sale. Cut the pockets out and store for reference. Patch, flap and jetted pockets are the most widely used.

'Black is modest and arrogant at the same time. Black is lazy and easy - but mysterious. But above all, black says this: I don't bother you - don't bother me.'

YOHJI YAMAMOTO

ALWAYS DEVELOP YOUR INITIAL DESIGN IDEAS.

Inspired by your research material, you will
begin to sketch ideas for garments and outfits.
These ideas are often spontaneous and raw but they
provide a starting point for further consideration and
development. Aim to develop between five and ten
variations from your initial ideas. Consider changes
in hems, details, fabric combinations, seams, darts
and so on. Sometimes your initial ideas are your best
ideas, but you won't know this until you engage in
the design development process.

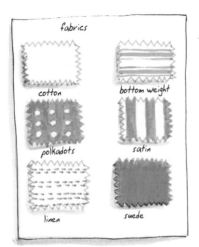

fabrics

cotton

bottom weight

polkadots

satin

linen

suede

✔

fabrics

cotton

bottom weight

polkadots

satin

FIND EFFECTIVE WAYS TO SHOWCASE FABRIC SWATCHES ON YOUR FINISHED SHEETS.

Fabric swatches can fray and often look messy, so time spent developing your own unique way of presenting them will demonstrate your attention to detail.

'There is no better designer than nature.'

ALEXANDER MCQUEEN

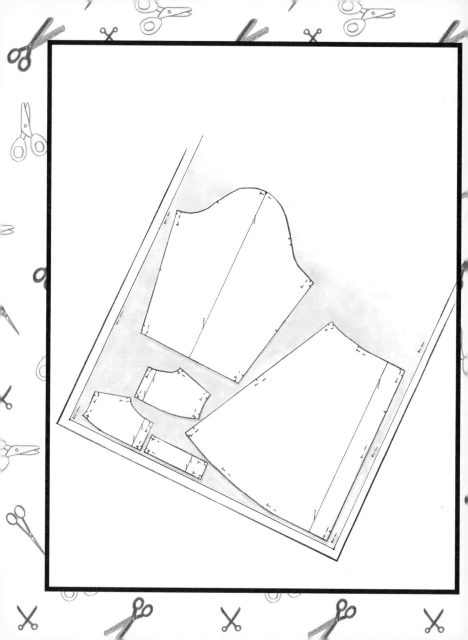

CUTTING CHIFFON CAN BE VERY TRICKY.

Secure a piece of pattern-cutting paper under a piece of chiffon using dressmaker pins, making sure that the grain line stays straight. Then place pattern pieces over the fabric, securing with pins, and cut using sharp scissors.

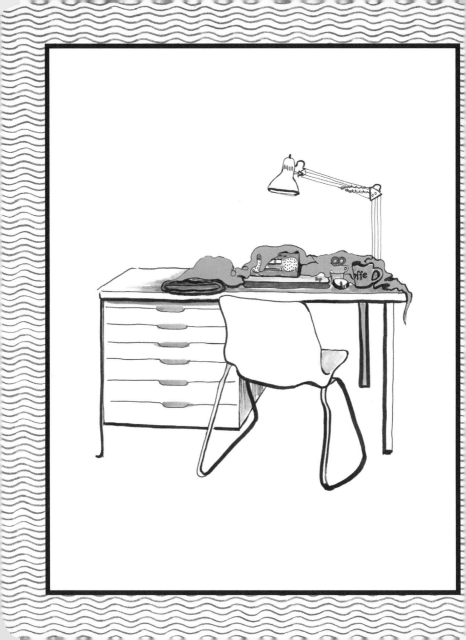

39

MAKE SURE YOUR PATTERN-CUTTING TABLE SURFACE IS SMOOTH AND CLEAR OF MISCELLANEOUS ITEMS BEFORE CUTTING YOUR FABRIC.

Also be careful to remove any stray dressmakers pins, needles and other small objects. This is because the straight grain of a flat piece of fabric can be set off course if not against a flat surface.

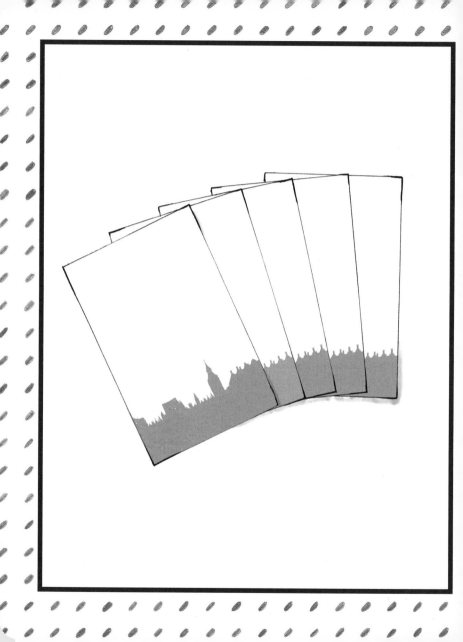

CREATING A TEMPLATE FOR YOUR FINAL PRESENTATION SHEETS CAN MAKE A STRONG FIRST IMPRESSION.

A fashion collection, by its very name, suggests cohesion, a common thread, and a sense of unity. A template really helps with this by making a project stand out as a considered body of work.

'Buy less, choose well and do it yourself!'

VIVIENNE WESTWOOD

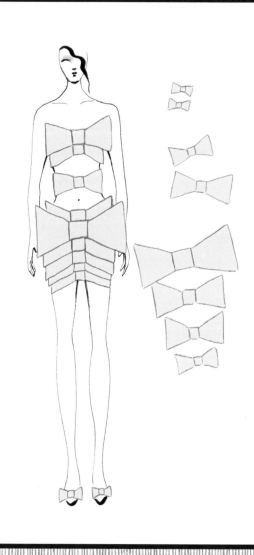

HOW TO USE A PHOTOCOPIER IN A CREATIVE WAY.

During the research and development stages of a design project, you will find yourself exploring proportion and silhouette. A great way to do this is by experimenting with scale and proportion on the photocopier – simply reduce or increase the scale by different percentages. Then by working with collage you can create new and interesting silhouettes.

43

GO WINDOW-SHOPPING.

This can be very useful research. Firstly, it will
give you a valuable insight into the different
levels within the fashion market – luxury brands,
designer, high street, independent and superstore
– by allowing you to get up-close and personal,
impossible when looking at magazines. Secondly, it
will enhance your knowledge of contemporary (and
vintage) fashion. Always try on garments, paying
special attention to fit and cut. Look at the fabric
label and the price tag. Window-shopping
can provide a wealth of useful information.

44

PLACE PATTERN PIECES WITH THE PILE GOING IN THE SAME DIRECTION,

otherwise you will end up with a patchwork of light and shade. Velvet has a pile (nap) that is directional. If you stroke velvet in one direction it will feel smooth (the nap is running down). If you stroke it in the opposite direction it will feel rough to the touch (the nap is running up). There is also a visual difference: in the first instance the velvet will appear lighter and shinier, in the latter richer and darker. Be mindful of this when laying out your pattern pieces. Mark your pattern pieces with an arrow to make this easier.

45

LIMIT ERASER USE IN SKETCHBOOKS. INSTEAD DRAW OVER YOUR MISTAKES, AS THIS HELPS YOU TO SEE WHERE YOU WENT WRONG.

Using a different media or different colour to do this will provide more clarity. Really take time to make an evaluative assessment. Where have you gone wrong? What can you do to provide more likeness to your interpretation?

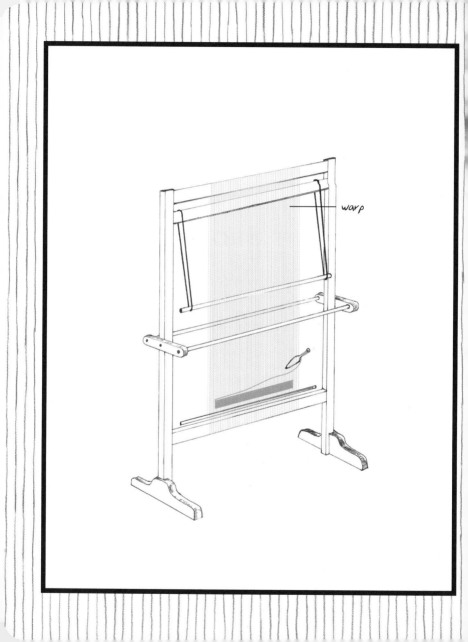

warp

THE WARP OF THE FABRIC RUNS IN THE DIRECTION OF THE GRAIN LINE.

The warp consists of the long threads that are stretched over a loom. A loom is used to create woven fabric.

'Style is knowing
who you are, what
you want to say, and
not giving a damn.'

ORSON WELLS

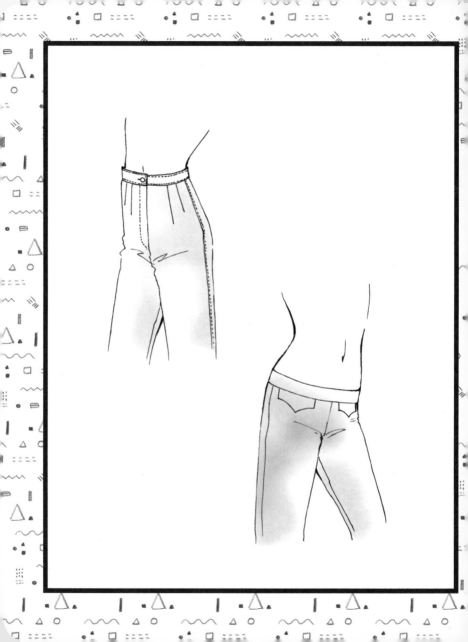

PROPORTION.

This relates to how the silhouette of a garment or outfit is broken up and how the different parts inter-relate. For example, the proportions of a pair of high-waisted pants are different to those of a pair of hipsters.

ALWAYS WIPE YOUR PORTFOLIO BEFORE SUBMISSION DEADLINE OR PRESENTATION.

This might mean cleaning inside the plastic sheets as well as the outside. Chalks, pastels, soft pencils and charcoal can often leave some residual on the sheets. Unclean portfolios are unsightly and distract from the work. They also suggest that you do not pay attention to detail and do not take pride in your work.

50

GET INVOLVED – HELP OUT FINAL YEAR STUDENTS IN CREATING THEIR FINAL COLLECTIONS.

You can learn a lot from this experience. Every academic year the final year students will graduate with a catwalk collection or display. This is a busy time for them and they will appreciate any offers of help. By getting involved you learn the best haberdashers for sourcing trimmings, the best fabric shops for specific fabrics, how to work under pressure and much, much more.

ALWAYS REMOVE DRESSMAKING PINS AS YOU PROGRESS IN YOUR SEWING TO AVOID TRAPPING PINS IN BETWEEN LININGS AND HEMS.

Trapped pins means unpicking stitches to set them free – most annoying. Always be thorough, it saves time in the long run.

AVOID TOO MANY BLACK AND WHITE PHOTOCOPIES IN YOUR SKETCHBOOK

or it will begin to look like a scrapbook. A sketchbook provides a space for your inspirational imagery and design development rather than just a place for found images (a scrapbook).

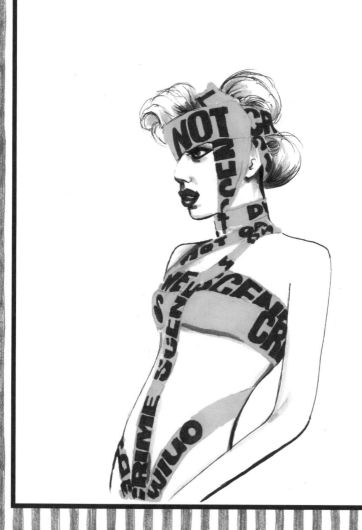

53

'I don't consider my own clothing to be outrageous... The truth is that people just don't have the same references that I do.
To me it's very beautiful and it's art, and to them it's outrageous and crazy.'

LADY GAGA

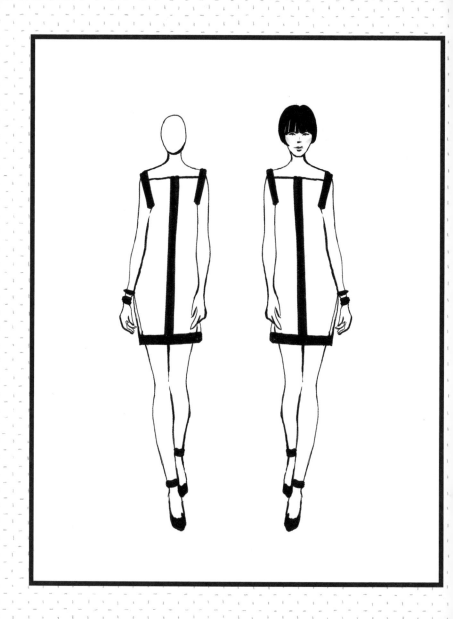

GIVE YOUR FASHION DRAWINGS FACIAL FEATURES – BLANK FACES HAVE NO PERSONALITY.

Fashion models have a very important part to play within the fashion industry. There is more to a model than being a clotheshorse. A face conveys facial expression and an attitude. A face, along with hair and makeup, helps to cement a designer's aesthetic. The face also enables the consumer to relate to a brand.

55

DIFFERENT TYPES OF COLLAR.

A collar is the part of the garment that frames the neck. Collars are typically made from a separate piece of fabric, unlike other necklines – such as lapels and revers – which are normally the same piece of fabric folded, or fabric that has been cut into. Collars can be found on coats, shirts, blouses and dresses. There are a wide variety: basic shirt collar, Peter Pan, sailor, Mandarin, shawl, tuxedo, Chelsea, pilgrim and wing, to name but a few. Choosing the right type of collar for a design should be done carefully, as collars can make or break a design.

56

BUY A SKETCHBOOK OR MAKE A SKETCHBOOK?

Can't find the right type of sketchbook in your campus art shop? Hate starting a new sketchbook? Prefer working on loose sheets of paper? If you answered yes, yes and yes, then making your own sketchbook is the answer. Creating your own sketchbook is not as difficult as it might sound. You just need to decide on the size, the orientation, the paper quality, the number of pages and the method of binding the pages together.

empty pages

57

BUY A SKETCHBOOK WITH FEWER PAGES THAT YOU CAN FILL UP WITH RESEARCH

for a project, rather than one with lots of pages that you only use part of. Is this trickery? Probably. It is, of course, always about the content, but as a creative, showing that you have an abundance of ideas goes a long way. Rightly or wrongly, a body of work that occupies half of a thick sketchbook might be viewed differently from the exact same body of work that completely fills a slimmer sketchbook.

58

ALWAYS READ AROUND YOUR RESEARCH TOPIC – BECOME THE EXPERT!

Understanding your topic and what underpins your interest is an essential part of researching thoroughly. Reading around your chosen topic can also open up new avenues of exploration. You will find this new knowledge helpful when presenting an overview of your project to your tutor – your delivery will be more fluid.

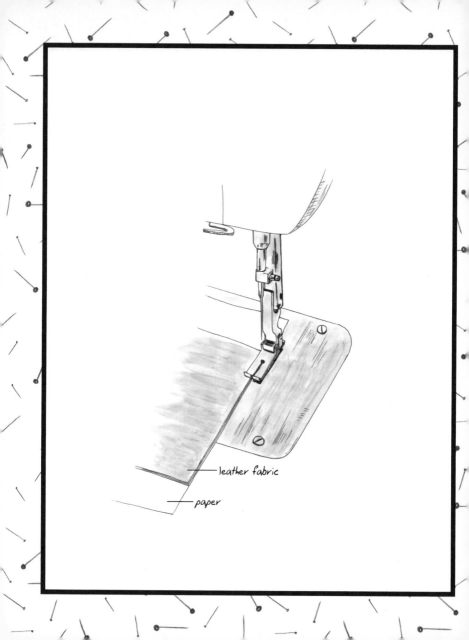

leather fabric

paper

59

PUT A PIECE OF PATTERN CUTTING PAPER UNDER A PIECE OF LEATHER WHEN SEWING IT

to help stop the leather (suede underside) from sticking to the surface of the machine. Place the paper under the suede away from the stitch line. You will certainly feel and see the difference when sewing – the leather will pass through with ease – putting an end to any initial frustration.

'The only real elegance
is in the mind; if
you've got that, the rest
really comes from it.'

DIANA VREELAND

DRAW, DRAW AND DRAW SOME MORE.

The old adage 'practise makes perfect' is very true. You will either be in the group of students that is happy with their drawing ability or you are in the other group that seems to struggle to get their ideas down on paper in a way that they appreciate. Whichever group you belong to, regular drawing sessions will greatly enhance your drawing prowess and confidence.

standard presser

zipper foot

piping foot

Teflon foot

right cording foot

62

HAPPY FEET.

When constructing a garment you will frequently
need to perform a wide range of functions, or
have to manage a range of fabrics to successfully
achieve the look of a professionally-made garment:
for example, inserting a zip, incorporating piping,
sewing stretch fabrics, sewing leather and lots
more. Your sewing machine can help you with
this as there are different machine feet for
different functions and fabrics.

63

ZIPS/ZIPPERS. WHERE'S BEST TO PLACE THEM ON A DRESS OR SKIRT?

Centre back or side seam are typical placements. But centre-back zips can be tricky to fasten – you don't have eyes at the back of your head! However, zip placement at the centre back (normally on a straight grain) is more straight forward (and therefore cheaper to manufacture) than placement on the side, which typically (due to fit) is not on the straight grain.

64

BEST DIRECTION FOR BUTTONHOLES ON GARMENTS – VERTICAL OR HORIZONTAL?

This will depend on the garment. Generally on shirts/blouses, the first button found on the collar stand is positioned horizontally, as are the buttonholes on the cuffs. The remaining buttonholes on the button stand are positioned vertically. On jackets all of the buttonholes are horizontal.

ART MEDIA SUCH AS CHARCOALS, PASTELS AND SOFT PENCILS WILL SMUDGE

unless you use a fixative to preserve and seal the image, stopping it from rubbing off onto the next page. Fixative should be sprayed evenly over finished artwork in a well-ventilated area

'I don't design clothes. I design dreams.'

RALPH LAUREN

STYLE LINES.

Also referred to as 'the line', these are typically
a boundary in the form of a line or curve that
distinguishes between two areas of fabric to create
a visual effect. Placements of seams and darts,
whether vertically, horizontally or curved, create
different effects as to how the body is perceived.

68

ALWAYS INCLUDE SHOES IN YOUR FASHION DRAWINGS.

It is fairly unusual to see clothed people going about their daily business barefoot! Drawing shoes also helps with proportion and styling.

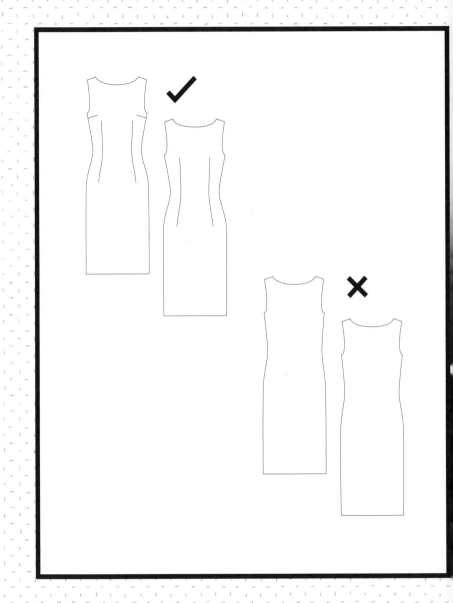

DON'T FORGET TO INCLUDE DARTS IN YOUR FLATS.

Darts transform a flat piece of fabric. They provide fit by simulating the three-dimensionality of the female form. They are frequently used in womenswear, such as bust darts and vertical darts.

LONG, NARROW SKIRTS EITHER NEED A SLIT OR MUST BE MADE WITH STRETCH FABRIC,

otherwise it will be very difficult to walk. Any fitted skirt that is just below the knee (a pencil skirt) and beyond will restrict movement unless provisions are made. A historical example of a skirt with restricted movement is the hobble skirt from c. 1910.

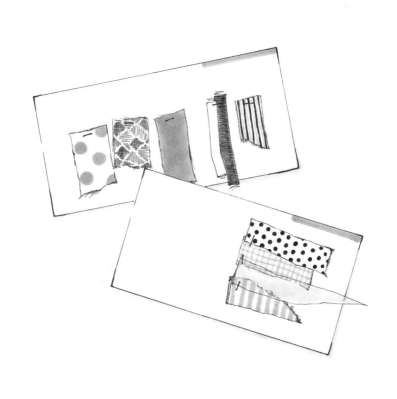

71

DON'T FORGET TO INCLUDE FABRIC SWATCHES IN YOUR SKETCHBOOK.

You need fabric in order to make clothes, so it stands to reason when documenting your research and development that you are also considering choice of fabrics. Fabrics have different weights, drape, and textures, all of which can be explored fully by making fabric sample cards.

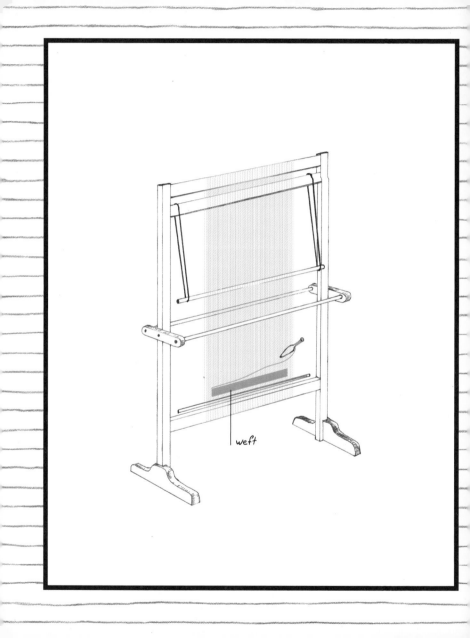

weft

THE WEFT RUNS PERPENDICULAR (AT RIGHT ANGLES) TO THE GRAIN LINE.

The weft consists of the short threads that are stretched over a loom. Different types of weaves – plain, satin and twill, to name a few – are dependent on how the weft and warp threads are crisscrossed.

'Create your own style... let it be unique for yourself and yet identifiable for others.'

ANNA WINTOUR

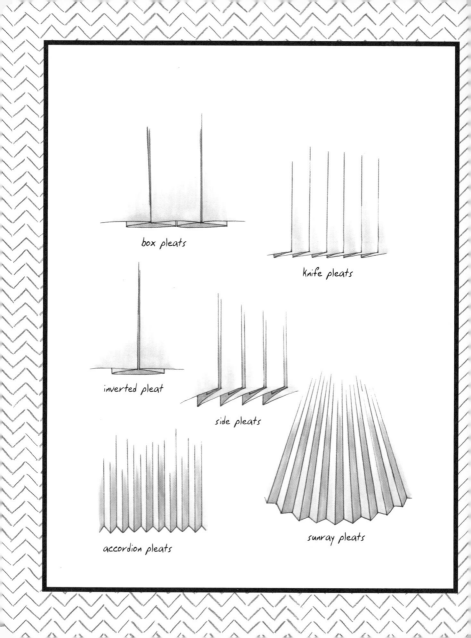

box pleats

knife pleats

inverted pleat

side pleats

accordion pleats

sunray pleats

74

PLEATS.

These reduce the overall length of a piece of fabric by various methods that entail the fabric doubling back into itself. There is a wide range of pleats, with box pleats, inverted pleats, sunray pleats and knife pleats being a few of the most popular.

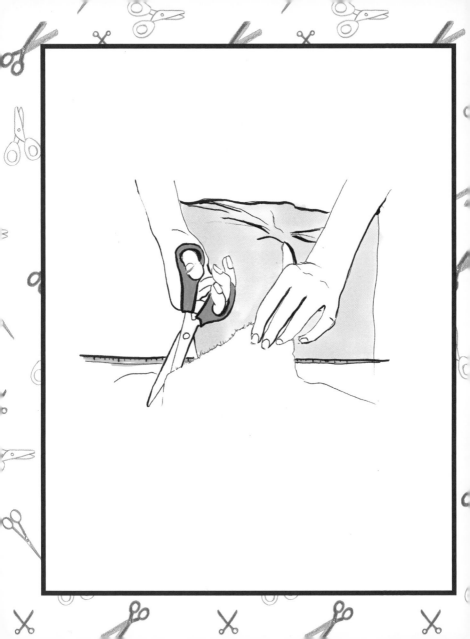

HAVE SEPARATE SCISSORS FOR CUTTING PAPER AND CUTTING FABRIC.

Sharp scissors are essential for cutting fabric accurately, but cutting paper blunts scissors, so have two pairs and keep them separate.

CREATE A TEMPLATE FOR A FASHION DRAWING

based on a model in a fashion magazine. Choose a model in a position that will help to show your designs off well. This will normally be front, profile and back views. Pay particular attention to the position of the arms, hands, legs and feet.

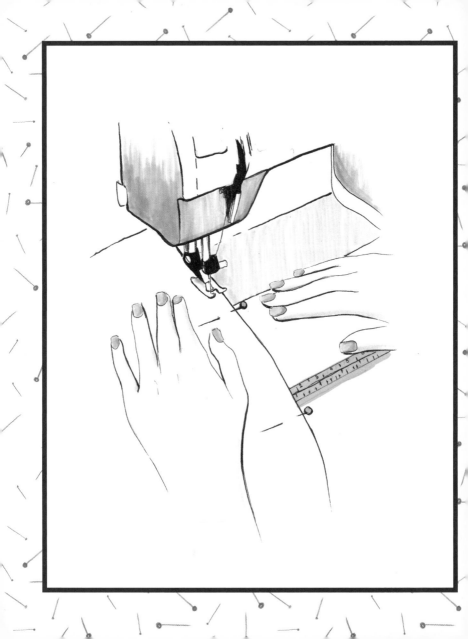

77

DRESSMAKER PINS CAN HELP SECURE PATTERN PIECES WHEN SEWING.

Who would have thought that you could sew over dressmaker pins and not break the machine needle? As long as the pins are at right angles to the stitch line the needle will not break. This is especially handy when working with slippery fabric, or if you are trying to match notches.

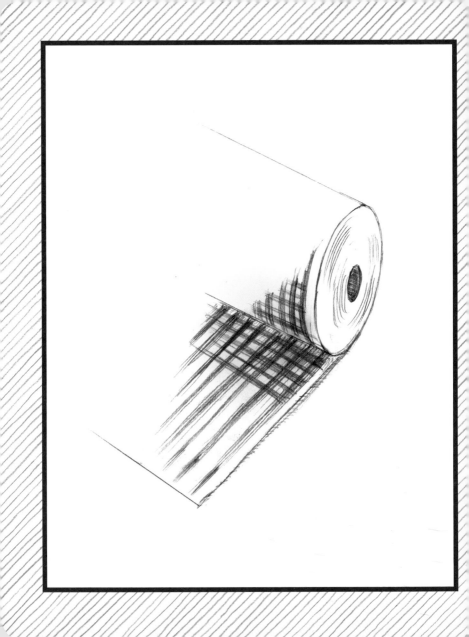

78

THE GRAIN LINE RUNS PARALLEL TO THE SELVEDGE (THE EDGE OF FABRIC).

Next time you are in a fabric shop, take out a bolt of fabric and roll out a length. You will notice that both outer edges are more densely woven. The outer edge is known as the selvedge, and it prevents the fabrics from fraying and unravelling. The grain line is always parallel to the selvedge.

'Fashion is a form of ugliness so intolerable that we have to alter it every six months.'

OSCAR WILDE

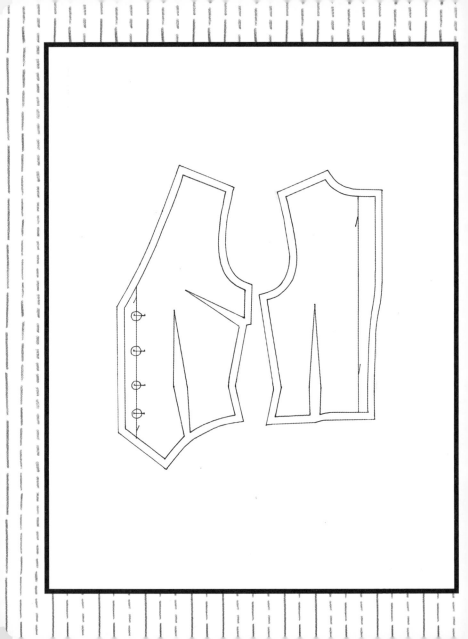

ALWAYS ADD SEAM ALLOWANCE TO YOUR PAPER PATTERN PIECES.

It is easier to make this addition at this stage rather than adding seam allowance with chalk to the fabric before cutting.

PRACTISE YOUR PRESENTATION WITH FRIENDS BEFORE ATTEMPTING THE REAL THING!

In fact, you cannot practise enough. Keep on practising until you feel comfortable with your delivery. This will help to take the edge off when it comes to the real thing.

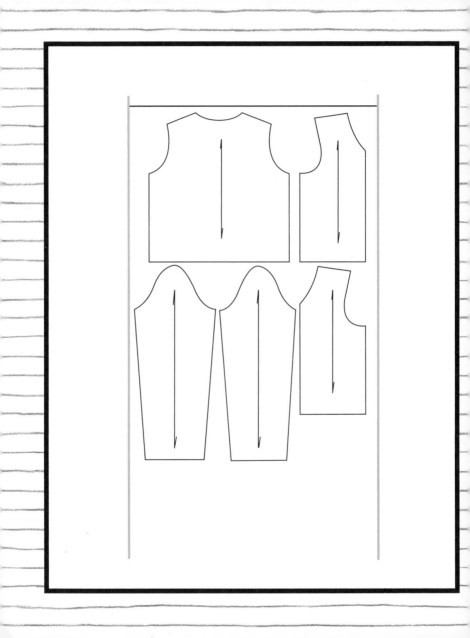

82

WHEN COLLECTING FABRIC SWATCHES, ALWAYS FIND OUT HOW WIDE THE FABRIC IS.

Fabrics come in different widths, which can make a difference to how many metres/feet of fabric you will eventually need to buy. Fabrics typically come in the following widths: 36 in (90 cm), 45 in (112.5 cm) and 60 in (150 cm). To work out how much material you will need, mark on a flat table the relevant width with chalk, pencil or a long ruler. Place pattern pieces economically within this margin paying attention to the straight grain line.

83

MAGNETS CAN HELP YOU TO COLLECT SPILLED DRESSMAKER PINS IN NANOSECONDS!

Tired of painstakingly trying to locate and pick up pins that have accidentally fallen? The days of multiple pinpricks are over – buy a large magnet.

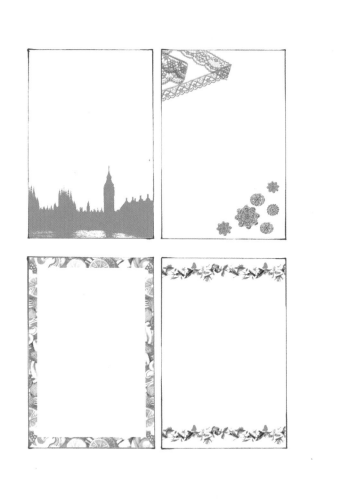

CREATE A DIFFERENT TEMPLATE FOR EACH INDIVIDUAL PROJECT IN YOUR PORTFOLIO.

This works very well in a portfolio. It shows that you are not a 'one trick pony' but are capable of unique and divergent ideas. Your aesthetic should remain the same, because that is innate, but you will be showing that you can package your aesthetic up differently.

85

'Art produces
ugly things which
frequently become
more beautiful with
time. Fashion, on the
other hand, produces
beautiful things which
always become ugly
with time.'

JEAN COCTEAU

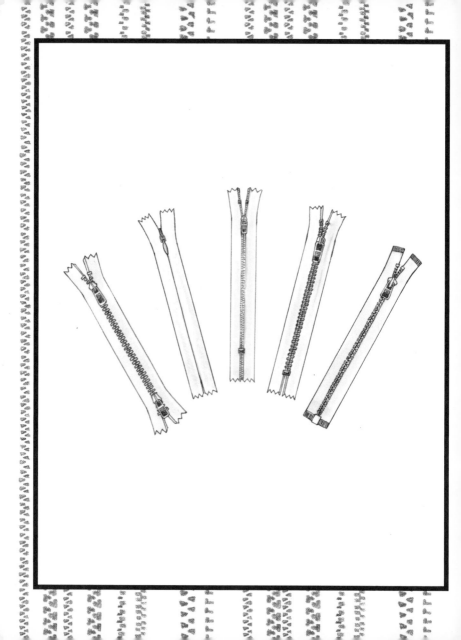

ZIPS/ZIPPERS.

There are two types of these: invisible and visible. Dresses and skirts usually have invisible zips in order to be discreet. The polyester coil variety is commonplace, as these don't rust and are lightweight, durable and heat resistant. Opened-ended zips are typically used in coats and sweatshirts. Metal zips are normally found in jeans – the teeth are made from nickel, aluminium or brass. Plastic-moulded zips, as the name suggests, are made from plastic.

87

COLLECT INSPIRING THINGS AND STORE THEM IN A BOX.

Always be on the look out for inspiration.
It could be an article in a magazine, a vintage
postcard, or even a pebble from a beach. Make
a special effort where possible to collect, or
purchase these items for your box. This box
of inspiration can become a place where you
can go to get your creative juices flowing.

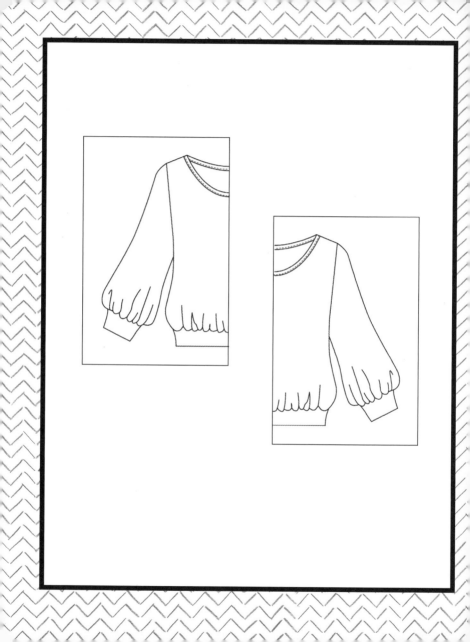

88

HOW TO ENSURE SYMMETRY WITH HAND-DRAWN FLATS ON LAYOUT PAPER.

1. Draw half of the garment on the vertical axis
2. Trace a duplicate on separate paper
3. Reverse the tracing so that you are looking at the mirror image
4. Place under the original drawing
5. Join both halves and trace over the mirrored half image on original paper.

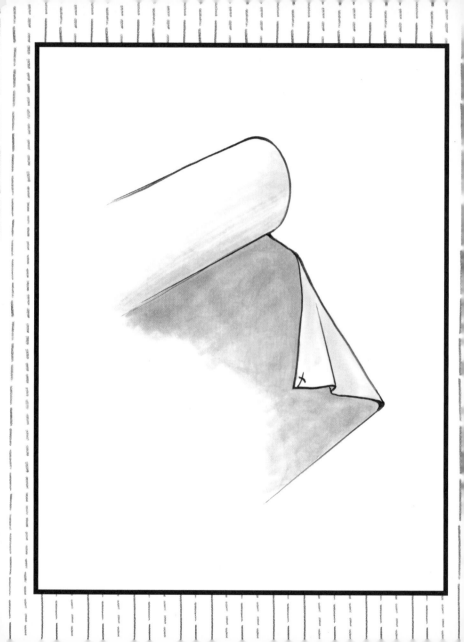

89

ONCE YOU HAVE WORKED OUT THE RIGHT SIDE OF A FABRIC, MARK IT WITH CHALK

so that you do not confuse it with the wrong side when sewing pattern pieces together. With some fabrics, distinguishing the right side from the wrong side is fairly easy – for example velvet, corduroy and boucle. Others are much harder to tell apart. Observing the fabric under good light and looking at the flatness of the weave at the selvedge will help you.

90

THERE'S NO SUCH WORD AS CAN'T IN FASHION SCHOOL.

Yes, you will find your course challenging at times; yes, you will wonder if you are cut out for the fashion industry; and yes, your own (at times unrealistic) expectations might prove debilitating. However, you are in an environment where all of the above (and much more) are part and parcel of the educational experience. You will frequently be outside of your comfort zone, but you will always be learning.

91

AVOID USING VERY SOFT PENCILS FOR FASHION DRAWINGS,

these are more suitable for art sketches. When producing fashion sketches or more precise technical drawings a fine line created by a hard pencil or technical pen is more accurate, especially for rendering small details such as stitching.

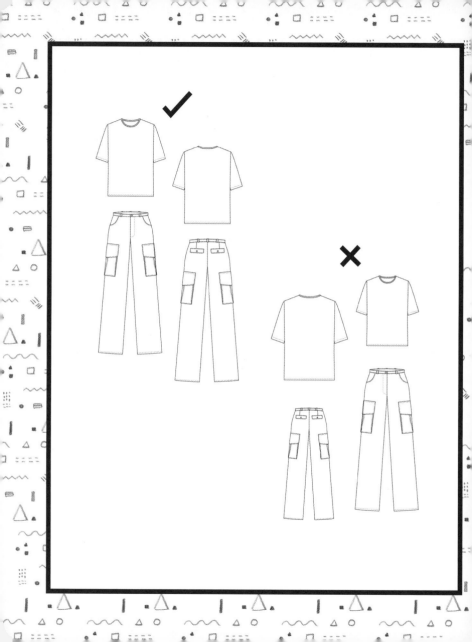

92

WHEN DRAWING FLATS, KEEP GARMENTS IN PROPORTION WITH EACH OTHER.

Your finished sheets will consist of coloured illustrations supported by flats and fabric swatches. Because you are not drawing individual garments in isolation but drawing outfits, ensure that the scale is correct to show how the components relate to each other. For example, a pair of trousers should not appear smaller than a standard sized t-shirt. Nor should a pair of hot pants be larger than a full-length coat. Tracing over your illustrated figure on layout paper will remind you of scale – keep this close to hand when drawing up final flats.

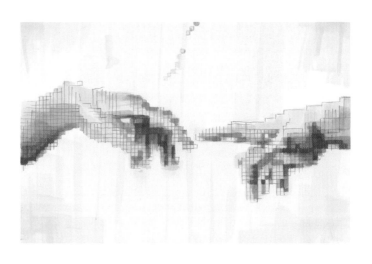

93

AVOID PRINTING LO-RES IMAGERY FROM THE INTERNET.

Quality should be evident in every aspect of your work in order to impress in the competitive world of fashion. The way that you present yourself, what you have to say, and the quality of your work are equally important in making the right impression. A sketchbook containing poor quality images shows a lack of love and is uninspiring. Well, even Michelangelo wouldn't have got far without attention to quality!

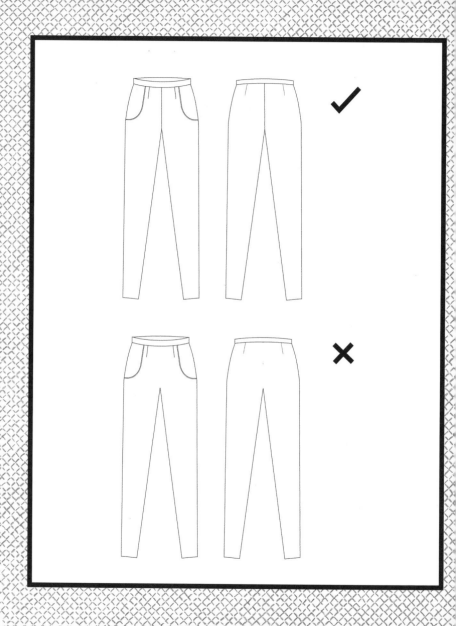

DON'T FORGET TO INCLUDE CENTRE-FRONT AND CENTRE-BACK SEAMS ON YOUR TROUSER FLATS.

Unless your trousers are skintight, they will need seams. Open your wardrobe and take a look at your own trousers: they all have seams, which are essential for comfort and a good fit.

International size conversions. Womenswear: dresses, jackets and coats.

S-M-L	XS-S	S	M	M	L	L-XL	XL
US	2	4	6	8	10	12	14
UK	6	8	10	12	14	16	18
Italy	38	40	42	44	46	48	50
France	34	36	38	40	42	44	46
Germany	32	34	36	38	40	42	44
Japan	5	7	9	11	13	15	17

Menswear:
suits, jackets and coats

S-M-L	XXS	XS	S	S	M	M	L	L	XL	XXL
US	30	32	34	36	38	40	42	44	46	48
UK	30	32	34	36	38	40	42	44	46	48
Europe	40	42	44	46	48	50	52	54	56	58
Japan	32	34	36	38	40	42	44	46	48	50
Korea	80	85	90	95	100	105	110	115	120	125

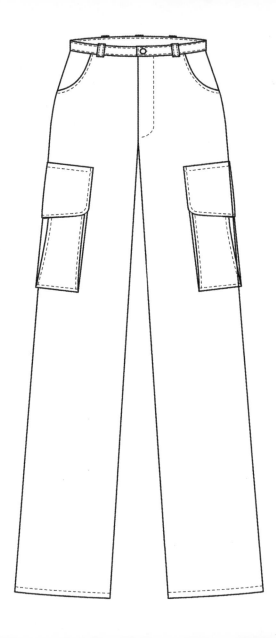

Menswear:
trousers

S-M-L	XXS	XS	S	S	M	M	L	L	XL	XXL
US	30	32	34	36	38	40	42	44	46	48
UK	30	32	34	36	38	40	42	44	46	48
Europe	40	42	44	46	48	50	52	54	56	58
Japan	32	34	36	38	40	42	44	46	48	50
Korea	80	85	90	95	100	105	110	115	120	125

Menswear: dress shirts

System	Neck size								
S-XL	XS	S	S	M	L	L	XL	XL	XXL
US	14	14.5	15	15.5	16	16.5	17	17.5	18
UK	14	14.5	15	15.5	16	16.5	17	17.5	18
Europe	36	37	38	39	41	42	43	44	45

Womens shoe sizes

International conversions													
US	4.5	5	5.5	6	6.5	7	7.5	8	8.5	9	9.5	10	10.5
UK	2	2.5	3	3.5	4	4.5	5	5.5	6	6.5	7	7.5	8
Europe	34	35	35.5	36	37	37.5	38	38.5	39	39.5	40	41	42
Japan -cm-	21.5	22	22.5	23	23	23.5	24	24	24.5	25	25.5	26	26.5

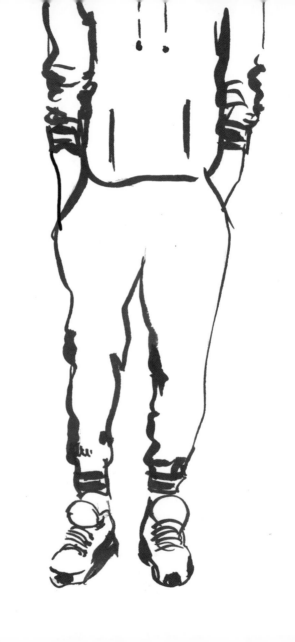

100

Mens shoe sizes

International conversions

US	6	6.5	7	7.5	8	8.5	9	9.5	10	10 5	11	11.5	12	12.5.	13
UK	5	5.5	6	6.5	7	7.5	8	8.5	9	9.5	10	10.5	11	11.5	12
Europe	38	38.7	39.3	40	40.5	41	42	42.5	43	44	44.5	45	46	46.5	47
Japan - cm -	23.5	24	24.5	25	25.5	26	26.5	27	27.5	28	28.5	29	29.5	30	30.5

EZINMA MBONU

Ezinma is currently Senior Lecturer on the BA (Hons) Fashion course at UCA Epsom. She studied Fashion Womenswear at Central Saint Martins and completed her MA in Fashion at the Royal College of Art, London, going on to produce her own fashion label. Ezinma has previously published *Fashion Design Research*.

ANNA HAMMER

Born in Poland, where she studied fine arts, Anna
now lives and works in Las Vegas, USA. Having
spent much of her career producing commissioned
portraits, she turned to illustration in order to build a
body of work for herself. Her beautiful coloured-pencil
illustrations demonstrate her love of fashion, and many
are available as prints and on merchandise.

Illustrations: 1, 3, 5, 6, 8, 10, 12, 13, 14, 15, 16, 18, 19, 21,
22, 24, 25, 26, 27, 29, 30, 31, 34, 36, 37, 39, 41, 42, 43,
45, 47, 49, 50, 51, 53, 54, 56, 58, 60, 61, 63, 66, 67, 68,
70, 73, 75, 77, 79, 81, 83, 85, 87, 90, 93, 99, 100

AYAKO KOYAMA

Ayako is a talented illustrator, designer and pattern cutter. Born in Japan, she studied fashion design at Sugino Fashion College in Tokyo and then at the London College of Fashion. Based in Japan, Ayako currently works as a designer for an ethical fashion label. She has previously created illustrations for *Technical Drawing for Fashion*.

Illustrations: 2, 4, 7, 9, 11, 17, 20, 23, 28, 32, 33, 35, 38, 40, 44, 46, 48, 52, 57, 59, 62, 64, 65, 69, 71, 72, 74, 76, 78, 80, 84, 86, 88, 89, 91, 92, 94, 95, 96, 97, 98